Just be Yourself

Written by Brad and Jim Tonner
Illustrated by Brad Tonner

ISBN: 099741250X
ISBN-13: 978-0-9974125-0-5
Library of Congress Control Number: 2016904543
Printed: North Charleston, South Carolina

We wrote this book for two
who are as different as can be
for Cynthia and her sister Leigh

Just be Yourself

Written by Brad and Jim Tonner
Illustrated by Brad Tonner

There's a mean ugly snake that lives near me.
She hides in the tall grass where no one can see.

She is green and has small yellow eyes.
Her tongue is forked and she hisses and sighs.

She slithers by every now and then.
Then she goes back to her dark little den.

Sometimes I see her bathing in the sun.
I run up and scare her just for fun.

We never seem to see eye to eye.

I guess, I never really try.

Maybe I'd like her if she
was different in someway.
If she wore a fancy hat when
she went out for the day.

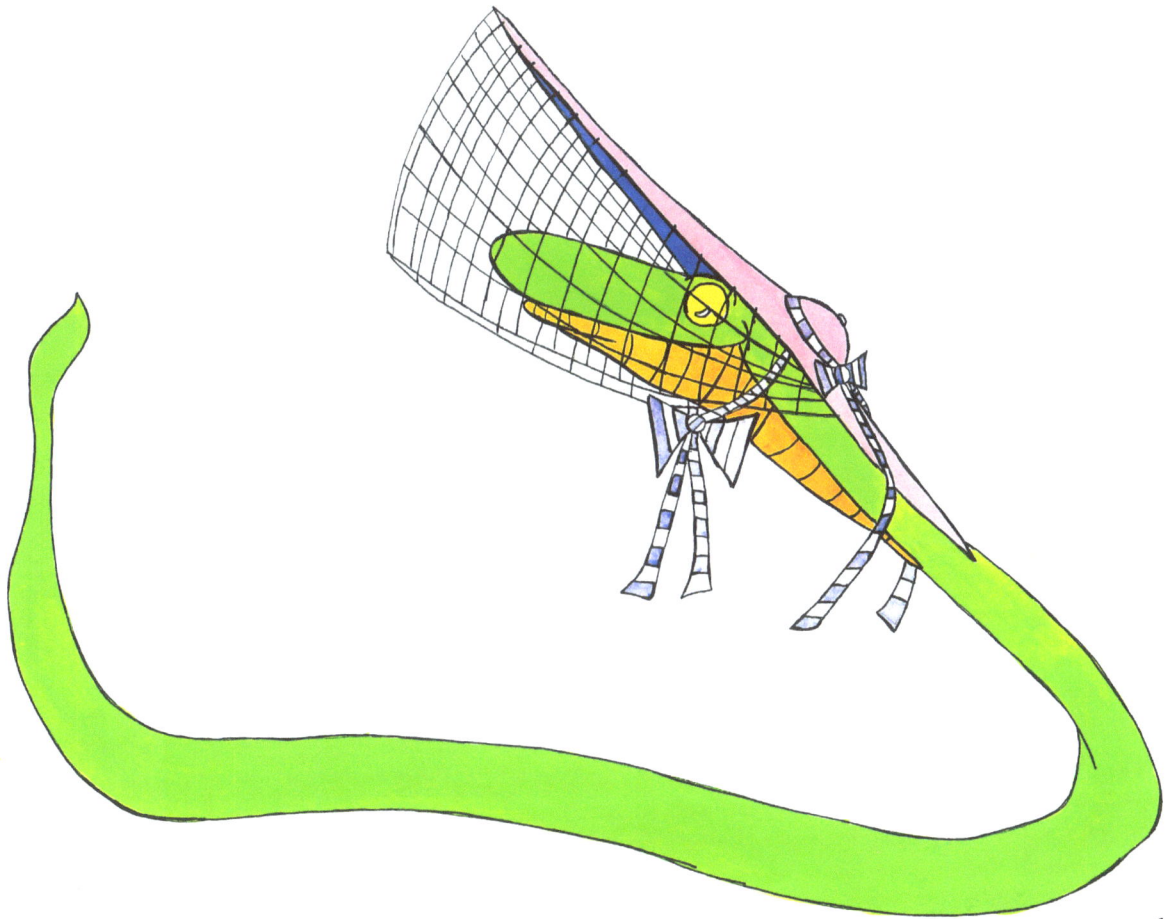

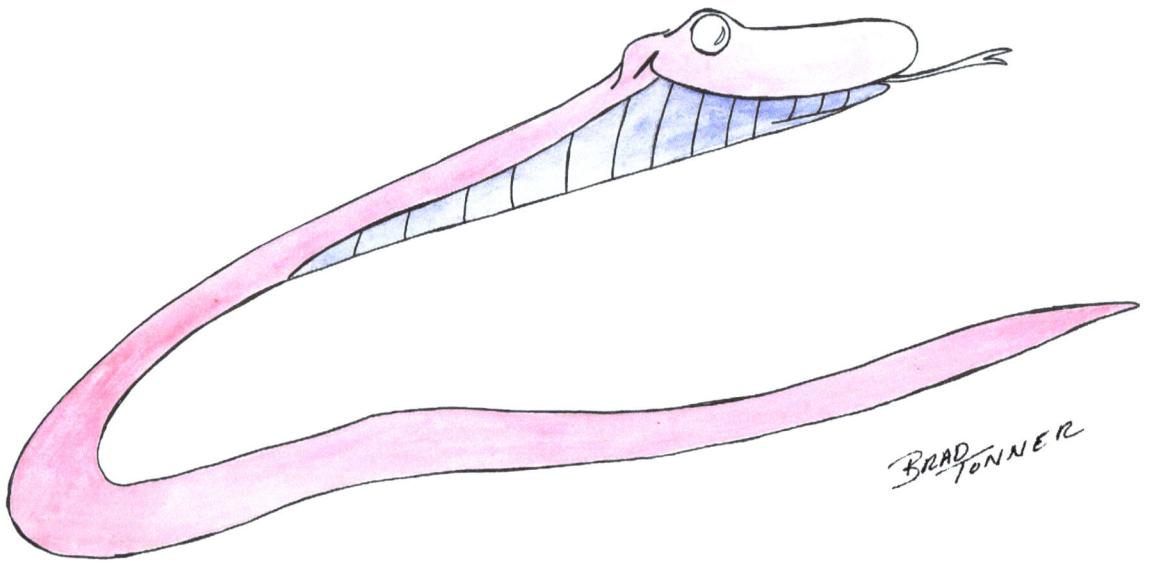

If she was a nice bright shade of pink.

If she used a fancy glass
when she needed a drink.

Maybe if she had a big umbrella
when she went out in the rain.

If she could fly a bright red airplane.

If she drove a fancy little sports car.

If she was a great movie star.

If she had a boat with a great big sail.

If she went to the beach with a shovel and pail.

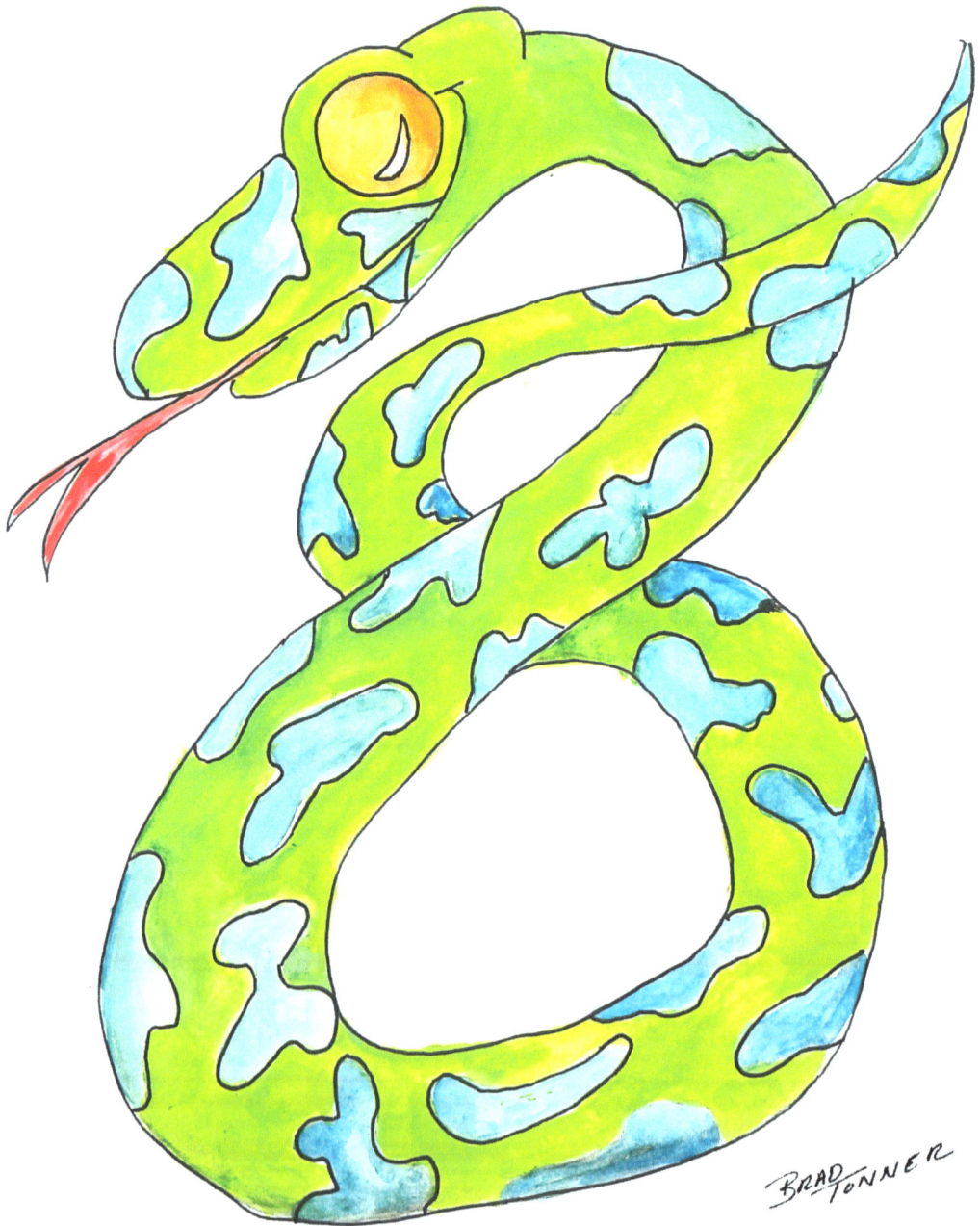

Maybe if she had big blue spots.

Or if she was blue with stars and polka dots.

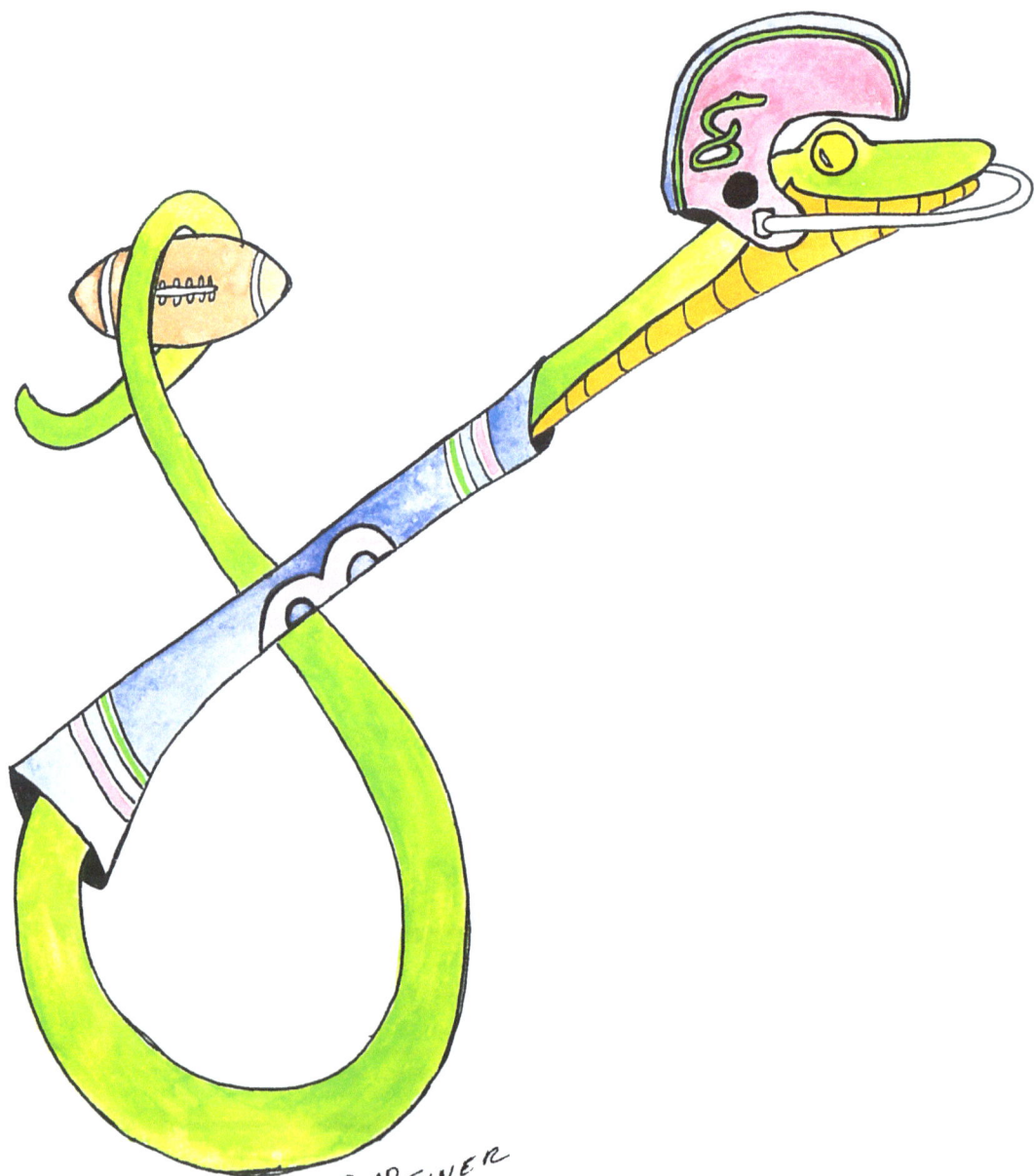

BRAD TONNER

If she could play a fun game.
Maybe, just maybe that would make her
seem somewhat tame.

If she would sit by the lake on a hot summer day.
Maybe I would like her that way.

BRAD TONNER

Maybe you can't change anyone a whole lot.
You can't be something you're not.

I guess, I can't change her that's the way
she will always be. She'll just be herself and
I'll just be me.

I guess what I am trying to say.
Is just be yourself every day.

www.ingramcontent.com/pod-product-compliance
Lightning Source LLC
Chambersburg PA
CBHW042100040426

42448CB00002B/88